BY DORIS DOANE • DRAWINGS BY RICHARD FISH

EXPLORING OLD CAPE COD

A PARNASSUS IMPRINTS BOOK ⚏ HYANNIS, MA 02601

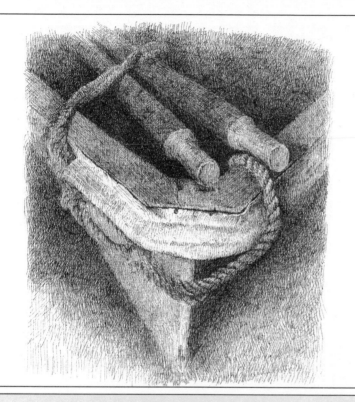

Introduction

Extending out into the Atlantic Ocean from the coast of Massachusetts is the "bold right arm" of this state — Cape Cod. Sixty miles long, with Cape Cod Bay on its inner arm, Nantucket Sound to the south and the great Atlantic at its outer reaches, the Cape is a place of great and varied beauty. It is many things to many people. For thousands of summer residents, it is vacation days filled with sunning, surfing, swimming, boating, clamming, fishing and just plain laziness. For an ever-increasing number of people, it is home, where a less hectic life is spent in rambling white clapboard houses or weathered shingled "cape codders," free from the city's traffic, noise and dirt. For the artist and photographer, it is hidden coves dotted with colorful boats; narrow lanes with trim houses behind picket fences; old wrecks abandoned high and dry on beaches; and lighthouses against the sky. For everyone, it provides a chance to absorb the character of early New England and to see many landmarks of the "firsts" in our country's history.

Where does the Cape begin? For most visitors, it begins as one crosses the Cape Cod Canal. Immediately beyond the Bourne and the Sagamore Bridges is the part the old timers call the *Upper Cape*. The *Lower Cape* extends from Orleans north to Provincetown. From the Canal to Provincetown, in addition to ocean beaches and innumerable fresh water ponds, quaint towns with their shops and museums, an Audubon Wildlife Sanctuary, an inland State Park, and the Cape Cod National Seashore await the visitor.

The Cape is a delightful area to explore, a place where one will be rewarded with the lovely and the unexpected.

Organizing Your Tour

This book is offered both as a traveler's guide and a pictorial essay on Cape Cod. The complete route shown on the map to the right covers the Cape in its entirety. The maps which follow show the important highlights of each town with a suggested tour outlined in white.

If you are lucky and your time is not limited, you may enjoy the grand Cape Cod tour that offers a comprehensive pilgrimage of some 150 miles around the Cape and back again. On the other hand, should your leisure time be limited, you can absorb the local color and see a fine sampling of the Cape's history and charm by selecting any group of towns and villages that are fairly close to each other, as so many are. In this manner, you are able to create a tour custom-tailored to accommodate your time, mood and pleasure.

Index to Town Tours

Atlantic Ocean

Cape Cod Bay

Nantucket Sound

10 PROVINCETOWN
9 TRURO
8 WELLFLEET
7 EASTHAM
6 ORLEANS
5 BREWSTER
11 EASTHAM ORLEANS
12 CHATHAM
1 SANDWICH
2 BARNSTABLE
3 YARMOUTH
4 DENNIS
13 HARWICH
14 SO. DENNIS
15 HYANNIS
16 MASHPEE, FALMOUTH & BOURNE

Cape Cod Canal

ROUTE 6
RT 130
RT 149
RT 28
RT 132
RT 134
RT 124
RT 137
RT 39

0 1 2 3 4 5 MILES N

1 Sandwich

Sandwich, dating from 1639, is the oldest town on Cape Cod. Prior to 1639, "the territory of Sandwich was embraced in a vast tract of land granted to William Bradford and the council of Plymouth."

SANDWICH CENTER

From the Sagamore Bridge, follow Route 6A about two miles, then bear right onto Route 130. This shady, winding road lined with many interesting old houses brings you to the Village Green and the center of Sandwich. Clustered around the Green are the famous Sandwich Glass Museum, the First Church of Christ and the Dexter Grist Mill.

SANDWICH GLASS MUSEUM

Here are housed examples of every glass pattern made in this factory from 1825 to 1888. Many people think the factory was started on Cape Cod because of the abundance of sand available here. Actually, the sand used in the glassmaking was imported. It is said that Mr. Jarves, owner of the factory, set up his business in a place where he could work a few days and fish the rest of the week. The museum is open from mid-April to mid-November.

FIRST CHURCH OF CHRIST

The graceful steeple of this early 19th-century church is considered the best copy of a "Sir Christopher Wren" spire in this country. Within this church is the oldest bell in America. Cast in Germany in 1675, the bell was a gift to the town of Sandwich from the grateful widow of a Frenchman, Captain Peter Adolphe. In the winter of 1702-03, when Captain Adolphe's vessel went down with all hands in Cape Cod Bay, the people of Sandwich gave them a Christian burial. The bell was sold to Barnstable in 1763 and was used to call the court into session. In 1963, 200 years later, it was returned to Sandwich.

From Grove Street, beyond the Village Green, the photographer, amateur or professional, can take excellent photos of the church with the quiet waters of Shawme Lake in the foreground.

DEXTER MILL

Grove Street is also a good place from which to view the Dexter Mill. Over the years it has housed many different enterprises, dating back to 1654. In 1961 it was restored to a working 17th-century grist mill.

HERITAGE PLANTATION

About a mile down Grove Street is Heritage Plantation, the former Dexter Estate, where the public may enjoy a magnificent display of rhododendrons, mixed in with other flowering shrubs and plants. There are museums featuring antique cars and other Americana.

HOXIE HOUSE

Returning to the Village Green, bear right and take Route 130 to the Hoxie House. Believed to be the oldest house on the Cape, possibly 1637, it was fully restored in 1959 and is now a museum. Its "salt box" design resembles the boxes in which salt was found in the kitchens of years gone by — a design adapted for houses because it eliminated the expense of a second floor and allowed winter snow to slide easily off its steep, sloping roof.

THORTON W. BURGESS

Opposite the Hoxie Museum on School Street, Thornton W. Burgess was born in 1874. He was the author of *The Green Meadow Stories*, enjoyed by so many children. Return to Route 6A by way of elm-shaded Main Street.

CAPE COD HOUSES

Before leaving Sandwich, observe the beauty of its architecture. There are graceful captains' houses, good examples of "salt box" design, and the well-known Cape Cod House. As you continue to travel Cape Cod, you will become familiar with variations of this style: the half, three-quarter, and the full Cape. Note the roof lines. Most have gable ends, but some have a gentle curve, known as a "bow roof." Maybe ship builders realized that this watertight roof design, in the shape of an inverted ship's hull, would work equally well in their homes on land.

SANDY NECK

Continuing on Route 6A, you will pass the lovely salt marshes at Scorton Creek. Turn left when you arrive at Sandy Neck Road for a mile-long detour that will offer you a spectacular view of high white sand dunes, found only at two other locations on the entire Cape.

2 Barnstable

The town of Barnstable stretches from Cape Cod Bay on the north to Nantucket Sound on the south, and encompasses several villages. As with other Cape towns such as Dennis, Yarmouth, Harwich, etc., the names of these villages often include "North," "East," "West," or "South," which do not always reflect those directional points on the compass. For this tour, do not be troubled by this discrepancy. On 6A, the first Barnstable village is West Barnstable.

WEST BARNSTABLE
This village is the birthplace of many famous men. Among them were James Otis, fiery pre-Revolutionary patriot, known as "the Patrick Henry of the North"; Lemuel Shaw, an early Chief Justice of Massachusetts; and "Mad Jack" Percival, commander of the frigate *Old Ironsides*. The Percival headstone can be seen in the cemetery near the center of town, on the south side of Route 6A.

WEST PARISH MEETING HOUSE
Turn south on Route 149 and after about one mile you will arrive at the oldest standing Congregational Church in America — the West Parish Meeting House, built in 1717. Here, James Otis led many a debate in

behalf of the Revolutionary cause. In the steeple is a bell fashioned by the Paul Revere Company about 1806. The church weathervane, a golden cock, five feet from bill to tip of tail, was a gift from England.

Across from the Meeting House is Church Street, which passes the former Parish House, birthplace of Chief Justice Lemuel Shaw. Shaw's father was one of the early ministers of the church. Church Street rejoins Route 6A and you may continue on to the village of Barnstable.

STURGIS LIBRARY
On the north side of the road near the beautifully landscaped St. Mary's Episcopal Church, where visitors are welcome to view the gardens, is the Sturgis Library, containing many fine editions of early works. It is housed in a former parsonage built around 1645, and considered the oldest building in the United States to be used as a library.

COURT HOUSE
In the center of the village, shaded by huge trees, is the County Court House; up on the hill is the County Jail. It is believed that the first deed on Cape Cod was recorded in Barnstable in 1689.

BARNSTABLE HARBOR
Just beyond the Court House, turn left at the traffic light and you will come upon a delightful harbor. It is reported that the Pilgrims intended to visit the harbor but couldn't locate it in dense fog and continued west on to Plymouth.

OLD CUSTOMS HOUSE
Return to Route 6A, turn left and almost immediately you will see a red brick building on the right. It was built in 1855 as a U. S. Customs House to process foreign shipping. It served as a Post Office from 1913 until 1959 when it was converted into the Donald G. Trayser Historical Museum.

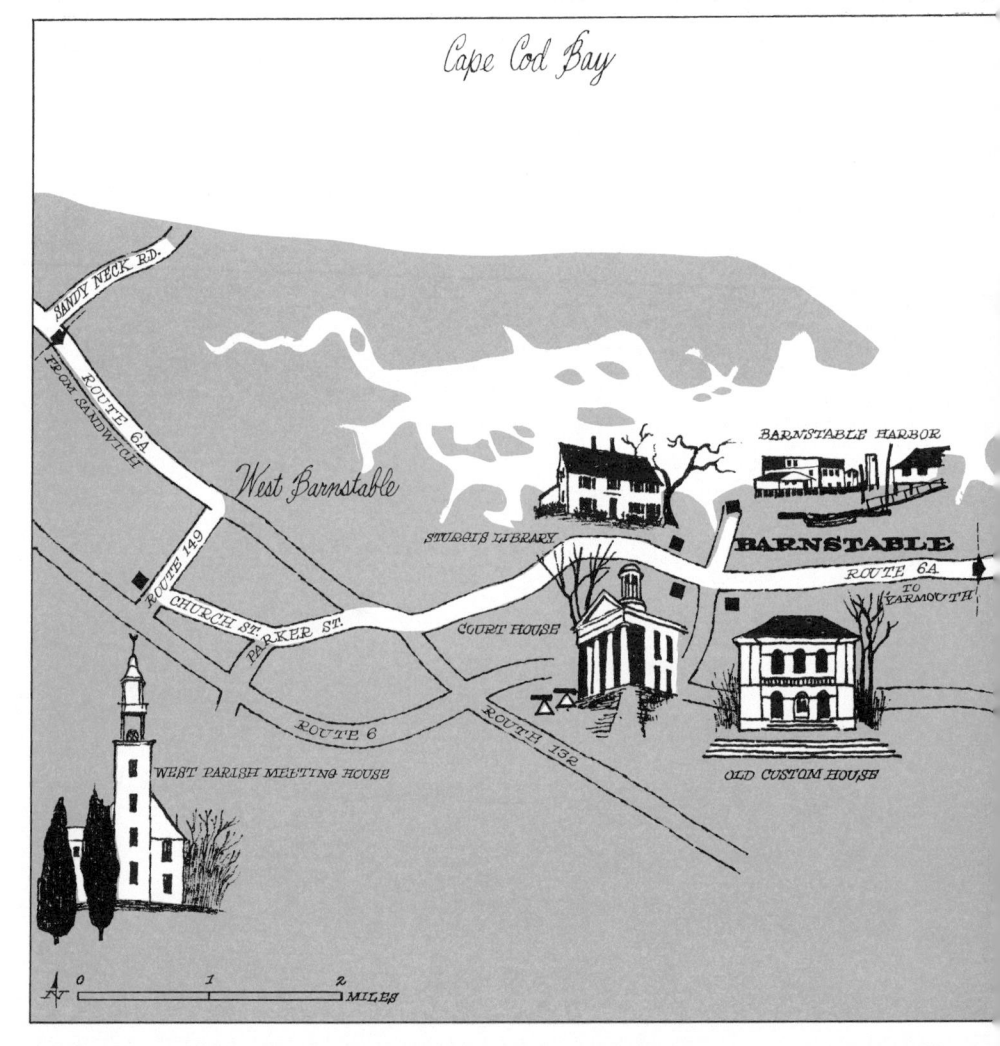

3 Yarmouth

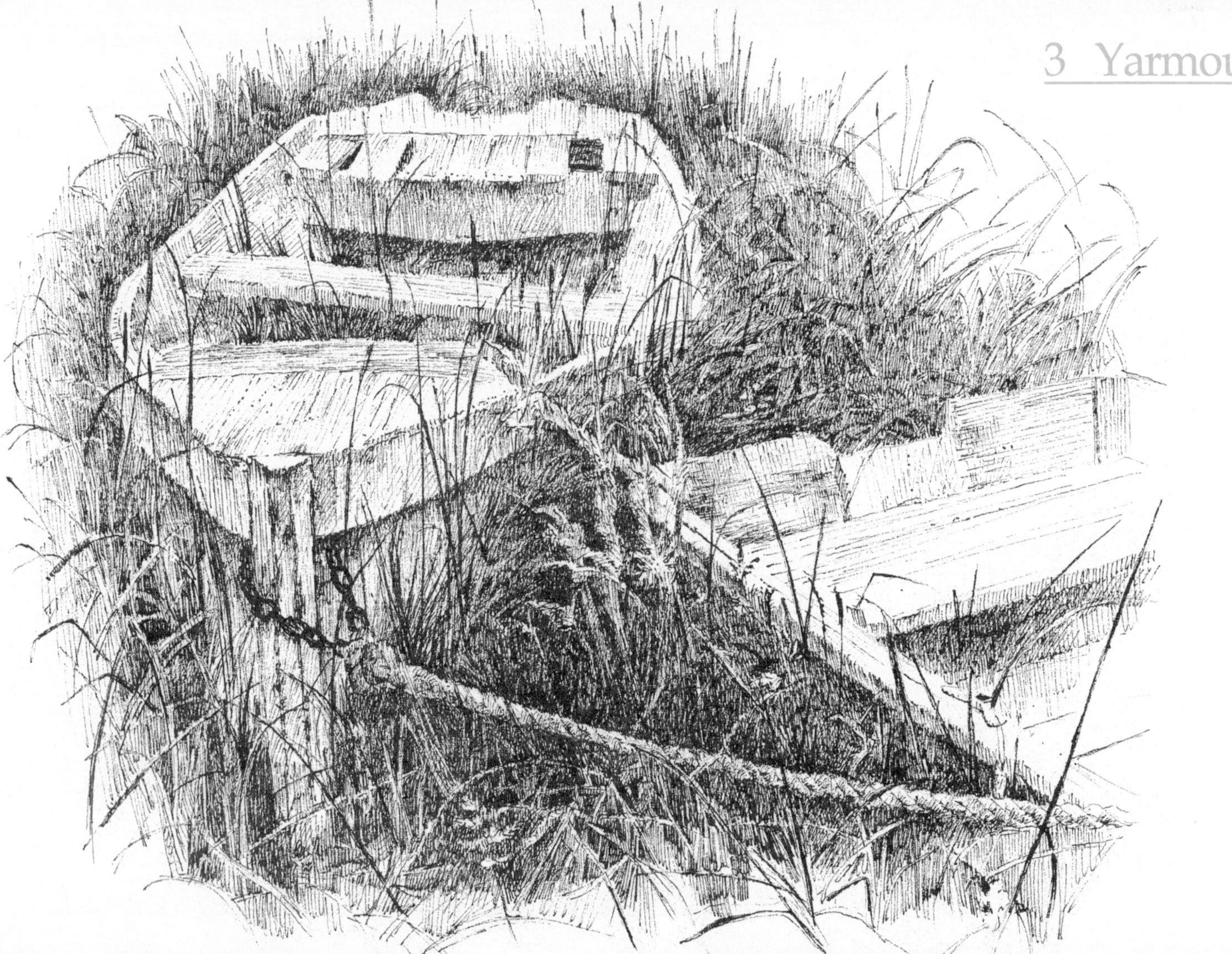

The next town on 6A is Yarmouth, which, like Barnstable, has many villages extending from the Bay to Nantucket Sound. Yarmouth Port is the first little village you will encounter.

YARMOUTH PORT

The main street, under beautifully — arched trees called cathedral elms, contains some of the finest examples of Cape Cod architecture. Here you will see the half-houses and the three-quarter houses previously mentioned and also the stately captains' houses. Among the many famous sea captains from Yarmouth was Captain Asa Eldridge of the clipper ship, *Red Jacket*. In 1856, he sailed from Liverpool to New York in 13 days and 7 hours, a record which was never beaten under sail.

OLD STAGECOACH INN

In Yarmouth Port, on the south side of 6A opposite the book shop, you will find the former Old Yarmouth Inn. It was once a stagecoach stop.

CAPTAIN BANGS HALLET HOUSE

Among the lovely houses surrounding Yarmouth Port's Village Green is the Bangs Hallet House, now the home of the Old Yarmouth Historical Society. It is open to visitors during the summer.

SALT MARSHES AND TIDAL RIVER

Before leaving Yarmouth, turn north on Old Church Street, at the yellow traffic blinker, and drive the short distance to the Bay. In July and August, the salt marshes are filled with glorious hibiscus (commonly known as "marshmallows"). As you cross a wooden bridge to reach the beach beyond, you will see a good example of a tidal river. This little side trip, and others like it, will permit the visitor to see some of the natural beauty of the Cape that might otherwise be lost to the traveler who whizzes down the mid-Cape Highway.

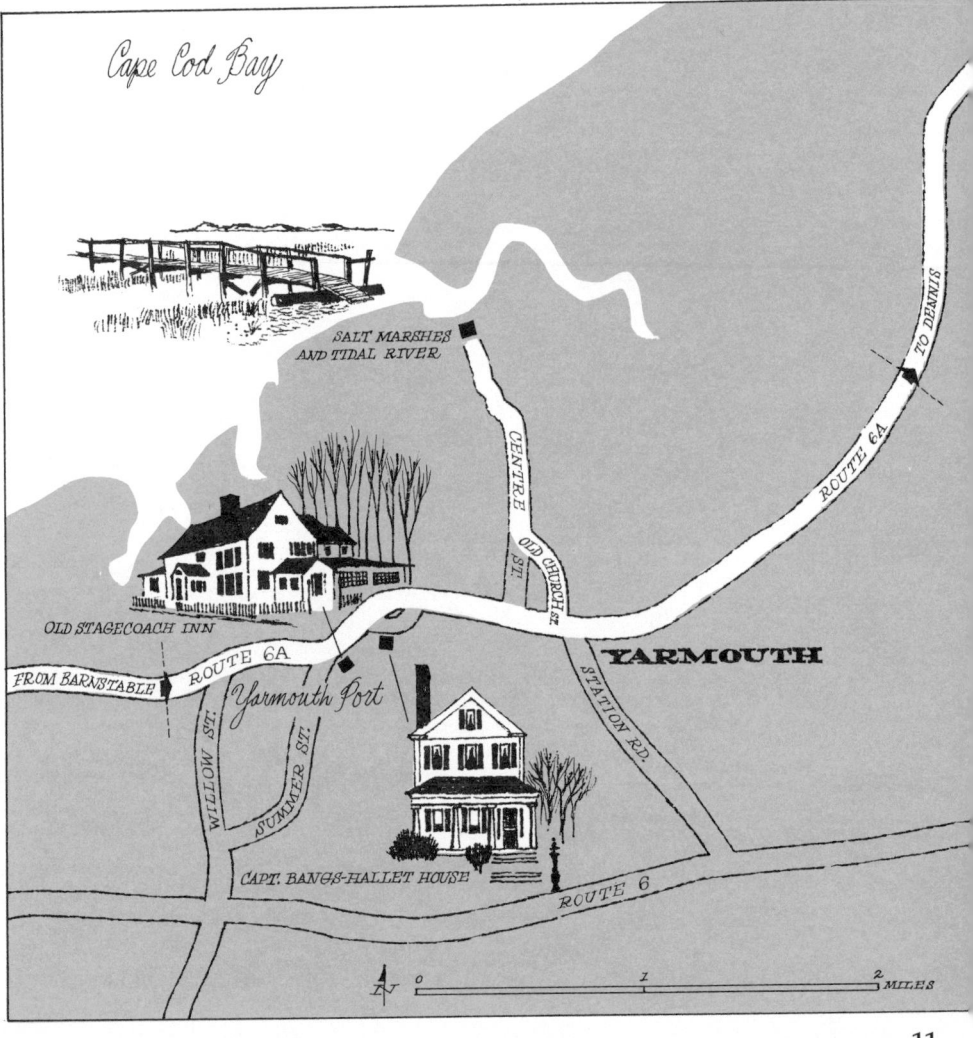

11

4 Dennis

Dennis, like the two preceding towns, stretches across the Cape from Cape Cod Bay to Nantucket Sound. Unlike most Cape towns, which were named after English towns or were given Indian names, Dennis was named for its favorite minister, the Reverend Josiah Dennis, who died in 1763.

VILLAGE OF DENNIS

As you enter this town, you see a Green across from which stands a small white country church, surrounded by a cemetery.

SCARGO HILL

At the Village Green, turn south on Old Bass River Road for a trip that will be well worth this detour of only two miles. At the summit of Scargo Hill, one of the highest points on the Cape, you will see a stone tower. The view from this tower is one of best; on a clear day you can see across Cape Cod Bay to the Pilgrim Monument in Provincetown. The tower at Scargo Hill is open daily from 6 am to 10 pm.

LEGEND OF SCARGO LAKE

At the foot of Scargo Hill, you will see a lake. Legend has it that many, many years ago an Indian chief had a daughter named Princess Scargo. The Princess refused to marry until a brave brought her a gift that pleased her. Many a brave tried, but all were refused until a candidate from a distant tribe brought her a pumpkin filled with goldfish. Princess Scargo chose this suitor as the one she would marry. However, when in a few days the fish began to die, the Princess became very sad. Her father summoned his tribe and ordered them to dig a pond for the fish. Armed with clam shells as digging tools, they dug until Scargo Lake was created.

DENNIS PLAYHOUSE AND CINEMA

Retrace your steps from Scargo Hill to Route 6A, and turn right. Just beyond is the famous Cape Playhouse, one of the early "straw hat" theaters, established by Raymond Moore. In the same compound, you will see the Cape Cinema, built to resemble an old Cape Cod church, even to the open horse stalls on the sides. The ceiling of the cinema contains the largest single canvas in the world — 6,400 square feet — executed by artist Rockwell Kent and Broadway's scenic designer, Jo Mielziner.

SHIVERICK SHIPYARD

This shipyard, opened about 1815, represented a thriving local industry. Today, by turning left on Bridge Street, and then taking the first right for about one-quarter of a mile, you will find a stone tablet commemorating its original site. Here, at Sesuit Harbor, many schooners, packets and clipper ships were built — ships that won world sailing records. The clipper, *Webfoot,* for example, sailed from Calcutta to New York in 85 days. The harbor is once again full of sails, but today they are pleasure boats which moor at the Dennis Yacht Club.

EAST DENNIS

Continuing on Route 6A, in the distance across the salt marshes, you can see the little village of East Dennis, once the home of many sea captains. East Dennis once boasted two lively enterprises; the Shiverick Shipyard and the Salt Works. If you wish to stop off and visit this quaint village, turn north off 6A on School Street.

SALT WORKS

In 1776, when salt was scarce, and taxed by England, a settler named John Sears devised a new solar method of producing it. He filled large vats with salt water and allowed the sun to evaporate the water, leaving a residue of salt. At first, the people looked askance at this operation and dubbed it "Sears Folly," but before long, hundreds of these salt works sprang up all over the Cape. The vats were filled by the action of wind-mills, which the ingenious Cape Codders, probably influenced by the Dutch, had built to pump sea water.

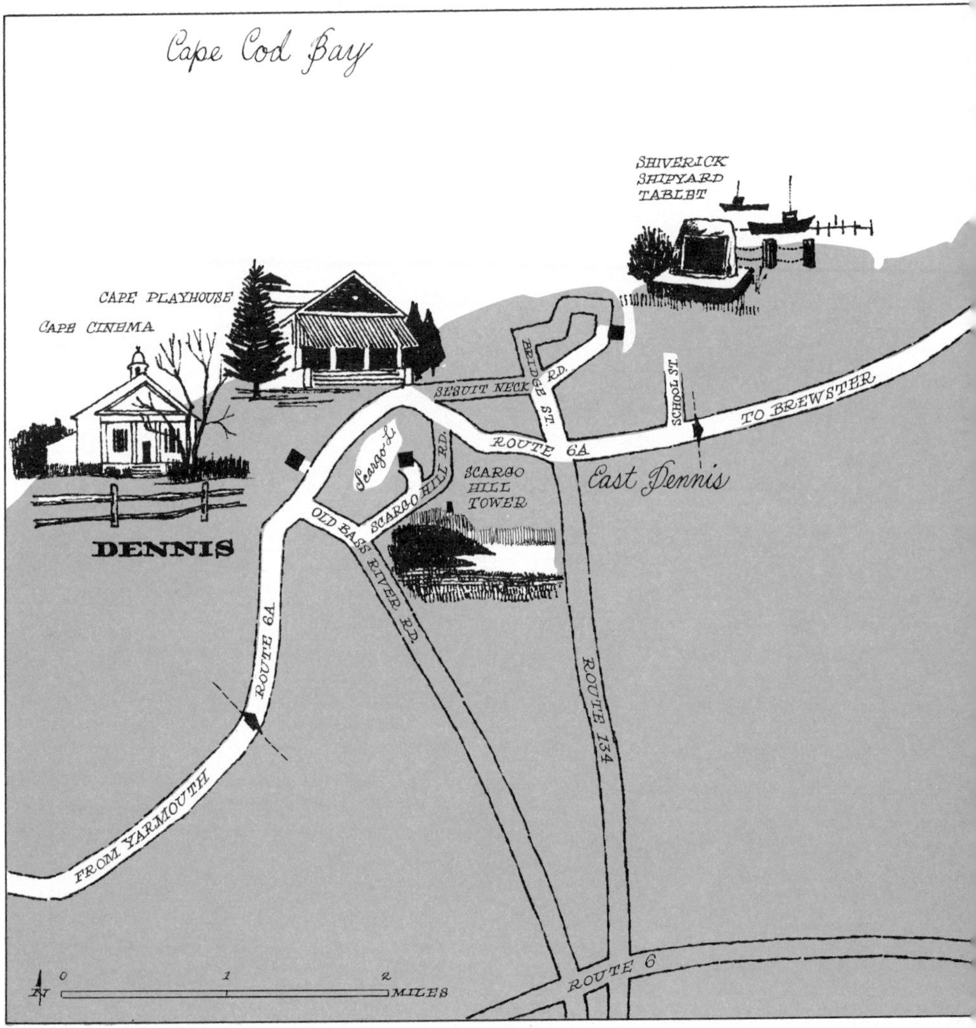

5 Brewster

It is reported that there were more deepwater sea captains per square inch in Brewster than anywhere else in America. Judging from the great number of large houses which reflected the affluence that only a sea captain acquired in those early days, this is probably true. Since most Cape boys went to sea at the age of eleven, many of these captains were masters of their own ships by the time they were twenty-one.

DILLINGHAM HOUSE

A little over a mile beyond the Dennis line on the north side of Route 6A, you will see the Dillingham House, considered by many to be the second oldest house on the Cape, and one of the best-preserved examples of salt box architecture. Most of the material used in this house was brought by John Dillingham as ballast in a ship from England. The interior has exposed beams and wide floor boards held together with wooden pegs.

CAPE COD MUSEUM OF NATURAL HISTORY

A short distance ahead on the north side of 6A stands the Cape Cod Museum of Natural History, which is under the directorship of very well-known naturalists. The museum offers a broad variety of natural history exhibits, including history classes for children and field trips for adults, conducted throughout the year over some 50 acres of salt marsh and high land.

OLD GRIST MILL

Continue east on 6A, and at the blinker, take a hard right onto Stony Brook Road for a view that will compensate you for doubling back on your trail. After proceeding about one mile, you will arrive at one of the loveliest old water-driven mills on the Cape. The first grist mill was built along this brook in 1663, and other mills followed until this area became known as Factory Village. The present mill dates to 1873.

Here you may wish to spend some time walking over the enchanting trails which meander beside Stony Brook, under weeping willows, and across rustic bridges. In the spring, the shadbushes are festooned with white blossoms, and you may see the herring or alewives swimming upstream to spawn.

This is also an ideal spot for bird watchers; over 50 different species nest here. For the botanist and wildflower enthusiast, there are over 200 plants to identify and enjoy. For the photographer and the artist, as for all who love nature, it is an idyllic setting.

ELIJAH COBB HOUSE

Stony Brook Road rejoins 6A. About one mile to the east is Lower Road, opposite the Baptist Church. The second house on the right of Lower Road is a beautiful Georgian manor with a widow's walk, built by Elijah Cobb, still another famous sea captain. In 1794, when Cobb was 25, his vessel and cargo were seized by the French during the reign of terror. After many months of being shunted from one official to another in quest of reimbursement, Captain Cobb finally took his problem to Robespierre, who granted him restitution. Two weeks later, the Captain was a witness as Robespierre was beheaded. Captain Cobb is also credited with starting the Wells Fargo Express in Australia.

LOST DAUPHIN

In the center of Brewster, in the cemetery behind the Unitarian Church, there was a headstone for David Nickerson. On this stone, the name of René Rousseau appeared. Whether or not there is any truth in it, a story has been passed down over the years that René Rousseau actually was the Lost Dauphin of France.

NICKERSON STATE PARK

Off Route 6A in East Brewster, there is a huge tract that was formerly a part of the estate of Rowland C. Nickerson. At his death, 1,950 acres was given by his widow to the Commonwealth of Massachusetts. It is now Nickerson State Park, a haven for campers, who are welcomed on a reservation basis.

15

6 Orleans

Orleans, the town beyond Brewster, was named for the Frenchman, Duc d'Orleans. Historians do not concur on the reason for this. However, in 1797, the year Orleans was incorporated as a town, the Duke enjoyed popularity as a champion of democracy and of the oppressed. Today, Orleans, with its shops and restaurants, comes closest to being the "metropolis" of the Lower Cape.

You may elect to see all of Orleans right now, or you may bypass much of it until the return trip "up" the Cape, via Route 28, when you may wish to explore the places of interest listed on pages 26-29 of this guide. If you do not wish to go into the center of Orleans at this time, turn left off 6A at the West Road traffic lights. Proceed almost a quarter of a mile on West Road and take the second road on your right. Now, follow the signs for Rock Harbor.

ROCK HARBOR

This quiet little harbor was the scene of a naval encounter during the War of 1812. The British were demanding a tax on the Cape-produced salt and though many of the towns reluctantly paid the tax, Orleans resisted. Its militia repulsed the British and drove them back to their ships. Rock Harbor was also the site of the Landing for the packet ships which plied between Boston and the Cape. Now the harbor is filled with fishing boats of many types.

When you leave the harbor, continue on the Rock Harbor Road for a scenic drive. After a mile's travel, you will arrive at Bridge Road. This delightful, twisting country road will take you past lovely old Cape homes to the Eastham town line.

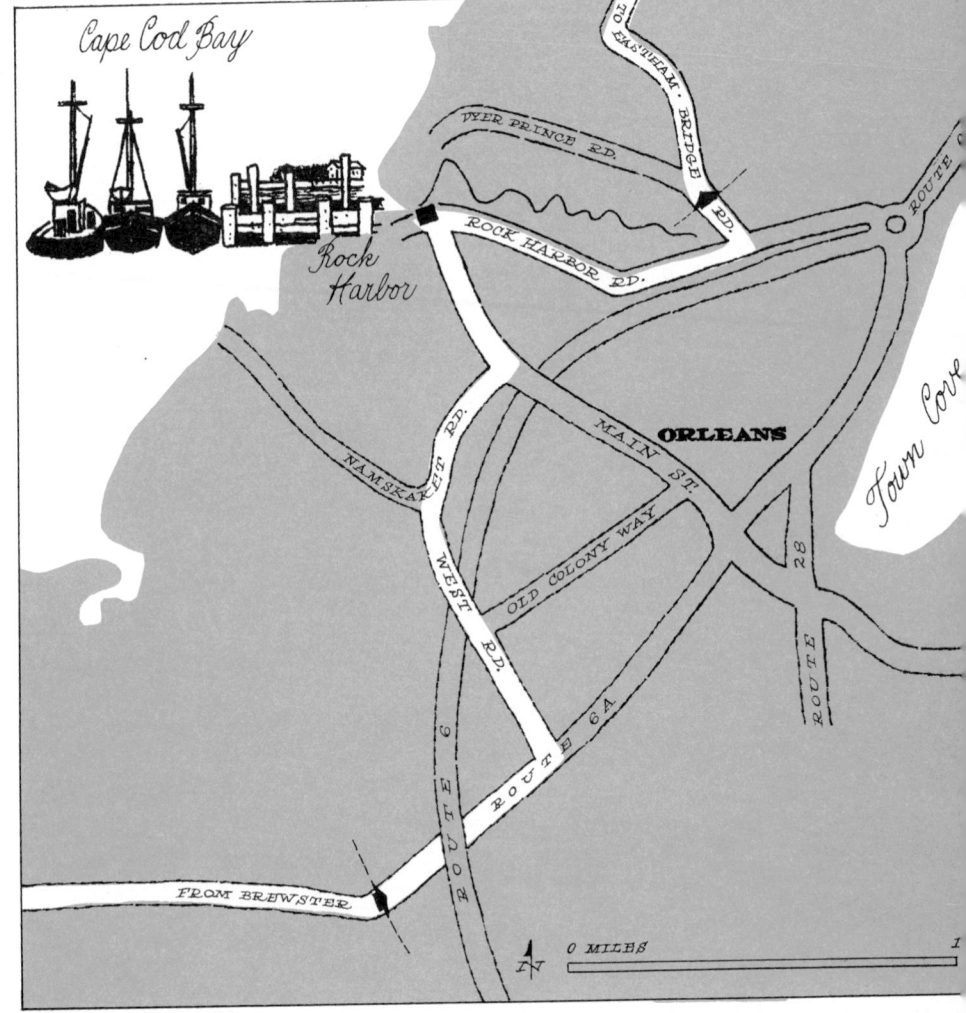

7 Eastham

Eastham was settled in 1644 by seven men who had been granted permission to leave the Pilgrim group at Plymouth in order to search for an area large enough to farm. At that time, there were no white men on the Cape beyond Yarmouth. One of the seven settlers, Thomas Prence, was chosen governor of Plymouth Colony in 1657 and governed the colony from Eastham.

BOAT MEADOW CREEK

On Bridge Road, you will shortly arrive at Boat Meadow Creek, which is shown on a coastal chart of 1690 as a clear passage from Bay to ocean. In the year 1717, Captain Southack sailed through to salvage what he could from the pirate ship, *Whiddah*, piloted by Captain Bellamy, and wrecked off South Wellfleet. During the 1800's, there was talk of establishing a Cape Cod Canal at this point, but the idea was abandoned because ships from Boston would still be obliged to pass the treacherous shoals off Chatham.

FIRST ENCOUNTER BEACH

After crossing the bridge, bear left onto Herring Brook Road and proceed to Samoset Road. On Samoset, turn left toward the Bay and the beach. It was here, back in 1620, that Miles Standish and his little army landed in a shallop launched from the *Mayflower* and first encountered the Indians.

OLD GRIST MILL

From First Encounter Beach, return via Samoset Road to Route 6. Just before you reach Route 6, you will see the oldest wind-driven grist mill still in existence on the Cape today. It was built around 1793 in Plymouth and was transported across the bay to Provincetown. Finally, in the 1800's, it was moved to Eastham. During the summer months, visitors can examine the workings of this mill, a reminder of the Pilgrim's former life in Holland. It is surrounded by a beautiful rose-covered rail fence.

CAPE COD NATIONAL SEASHORE

Leaving the mill, turn left on Route 6 and proceed about one quarter of a mile. On your right, at the traffic light, is the entrance to the Salt Pond Visitor Center. Here you will learn about the National Seashore and also enjoy one of the most beautiful views on the Cape. Before you lies Salt Pond, a kettle hole left by an ancient glacier. From the Atlantic Ocean, which is in the distance, a tidal stream winds its way through the great Nauset Marsh to feed this pond. The Center has an excellent museum of the Cape's historical legacies and natural history. The staff provides information on guided nature walks, outdoor exhibits, bicycle paths and many trails throughout the National Seashore.

SCHOOLHOUSE MUSEUM

Directly opposite the Center is the Eastham Historical Society, located in a restored building which was formerly the schoolhouse for the town of Eastham. It dates back to 1869.

COAST GUARD BEACH

The raging storm of 1978 eroded Coast Guard Beach, sweeping everything, including bathing facilities, in its wake. None of the nine cottages, which were on Nauset spit, are left. Check with the Visitor Center in Eastham for swimming information and beach use. The roadsides leading to the beach are covered with a low green vine called bearberry, and as you near the ocean you will find clumps of hudsonia, or poverty grass. About the first week in June, this heath plant blossoms into yellow flowers that transform the sand dunes into hills of gold.

NAUSET LIGHT

The lighthouse is about one mile from the Coast Guard Beach via Ocean View Road. In 1839, when the bluff extended much farther out into the ocean, three brick towers were erected on it. As the bluff was eroded by winter gales and storm waves, the towers tumbled into the ocean. Later, three wooden towers, called the "three sisters," were built to replace the lost brick ones. Soon, however, these too were in danger and had to be relocated about a quarter-mile west on the north side of Cable Road. The present lighthouse was brought from Chatham in 1923. It is shown on this book's cover.

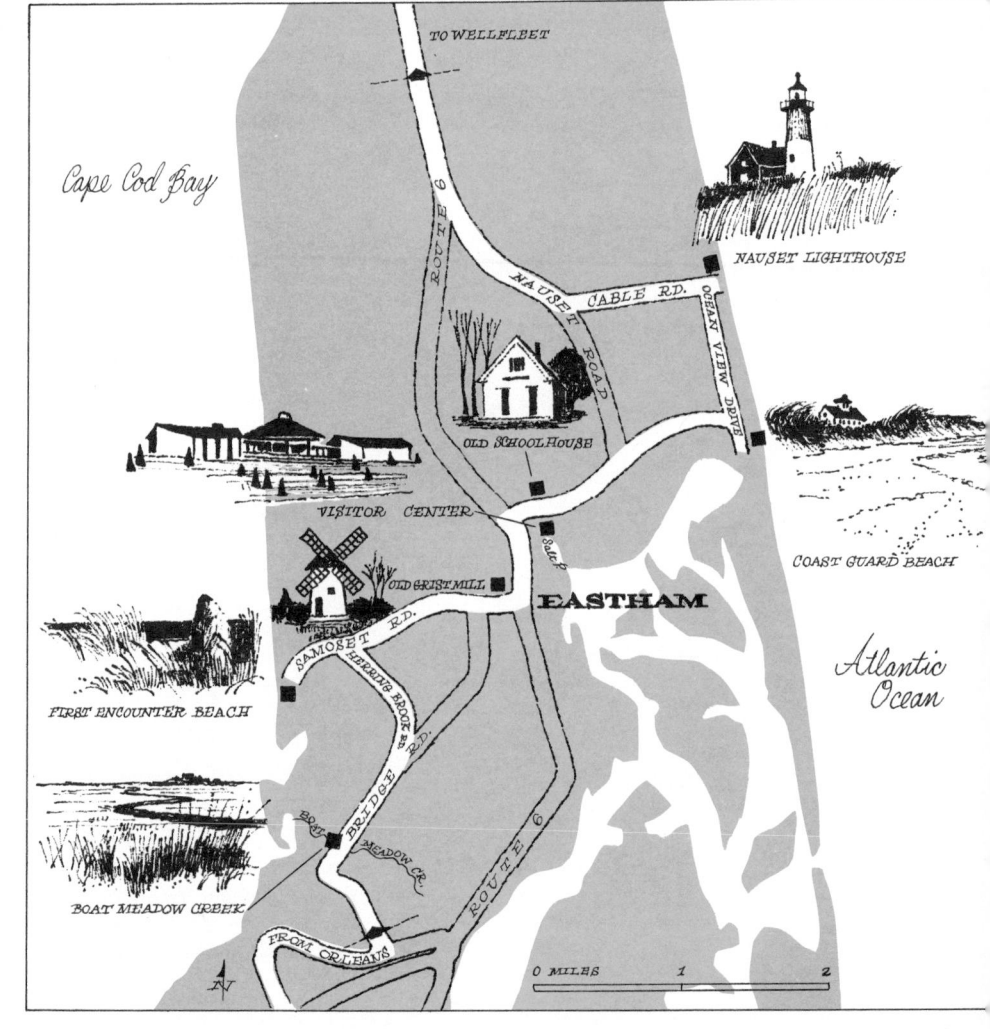

8 Wellfleet

Wellfleet has retained a great deal of the charm for which it was renowned when it was one of the most important whaling towns of the Cape. It is also known for its oysters, and is believed to have derived its name from England's famous oyster town, Wallfleet.

AUDUBON WILDLIFE SANCTUARY

From Nauset Light in Eastham, travel on Cable Road and Nauset Road to rejoin Route 6. Approximately one mile on the west side of Route 6 is the sign for the Audubon Society's Wildlife Sanctuary. This delightful area on the Bay side of the Cape is located in South Wellfleet. Here you will discover nature trails and many species of birds, too intriguing to pass by.

MARCONI AREA

Return to Route 6 and turn left. Two miles north on your right you will find the Marconi Area, now under the jurisdiction of the National Seashore. Turn right at the traffic light. On your way to the Marconi site, you will pass the administrative building for the Cape Cod National Seashore on your left.

MARCONI SITE

On a bluff, 85 feet above the Atlantic Ocean, is the Marconi Pavilion, containing a model of the Marconi Wireless Station. The original station was constructed in November, 1901, but before any signals could be sent, a storm destroyed its twenty 200 foot-high antenna poles shaped like ship's masts. In 1902, four 200-foot timbered towers were erected. On January 19, 1903, Marconi himself transmitted the first trans-

Atlantic wireless message from the United States: a message from President Theodore Roosevelt to Edward the VII, King of England. The station continued in use until 1918, when it was shut down.

SCENIC DRIVE

Return to Route 6 from the Marconi Site; turn right, and just a mile ahead on LeCount Hollow Road you will arrive at Ocean View Road, which affords a spectacular scenic drive. Ocean View Road runs high above and parallel with the ocean, which is hidden at times by beautiful sand dunes covered with bearberry, hudsonia and corema (a pre-glacial plant). The scenic road is about three miles long. To return to Route 6, take the third left onto Gross Hill Road.

WELLFLEET CENTER

Cross over Route 6 and wind through the center of Wellfleet to the harbor. About an eighth of a mile beyond the fire station, drive into a large parking area on your left. From this vantage spot, you can look back across a salt marsh at some old Cape houses nestled among the trees on a hill. An old church stands at the very top of the hill. The clock on this church strikes ship's time, possibly the only clock in America to do so. This is an ideal spot for photographers to capture the Cape's charm.

CHEQUESSET NECK ROAD

From the town pier at Wellfleet Harbor, turn right on a road that runs two-and-a-half miles along Cape Cod Bay; at its end, on the summit of a hill, one will be rewarded with views of glorious sunsets. Appropriately enough, the spot is called Sunset Hill. To return to Wellfleet, retrace your route almost two miles to the fork. Bear left, and this will bring you to Main Street. Turn left, going North, onto West Main Street which leads to Truro, about seven miles over a good hardtop road that winds through a variety of Cape landscapes.

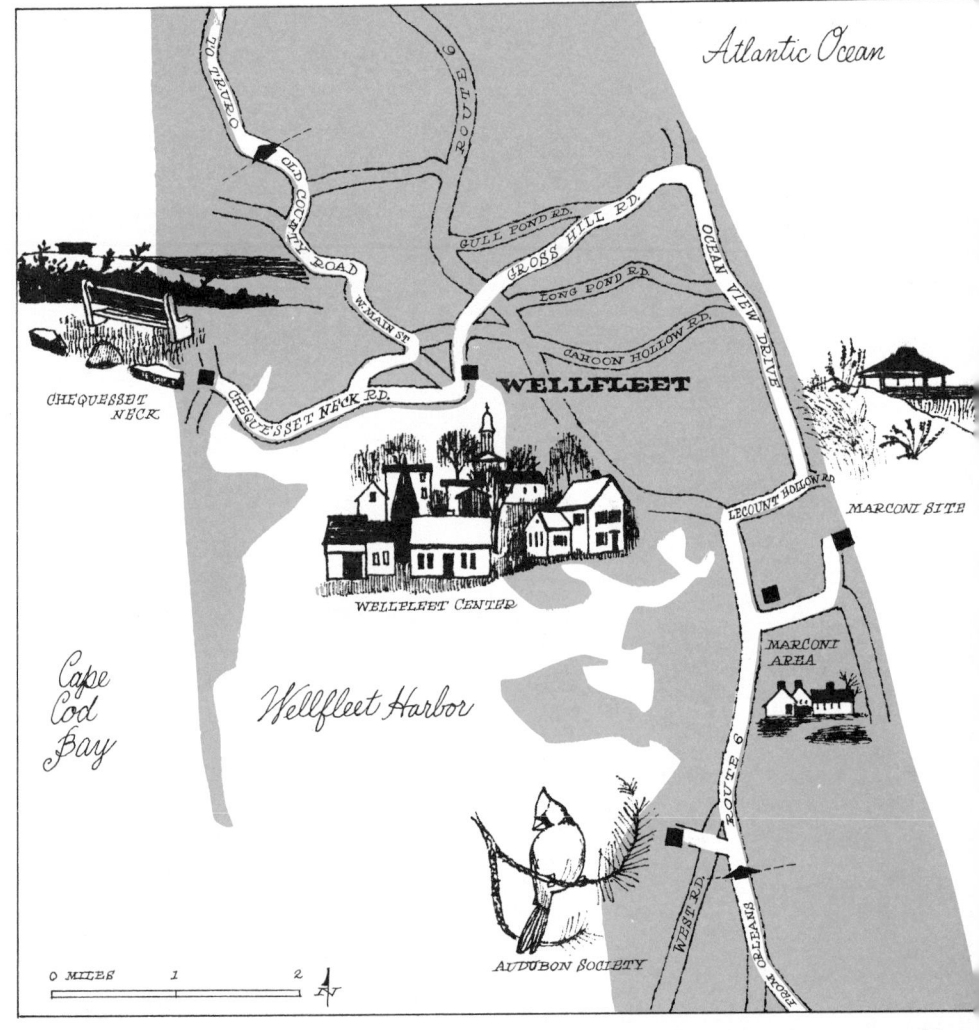

9 Truro

Truro is the Scotland of the Cape with its hills and dales covered with heath reminiscent of the Scottish moors. On Old County Road you can enjoy the town's wild, natural beauty. Here you will see wooded roads, marshes in the valleys, and you will climb rolling hills covered with bearberry until you reach a peak where Truro lies stretched out before you. It is here that you may observe more of the great kettle holes left by the glacier. On a dark, overcast day, with great clouds billowing in from the Bay, one is reminded of Sir Arthur Conan Doyle's novel, The Hound of the Baskervilles. This road terminates at the Truro Post Office. Now, turn left for Corn Hill.

CORN HILL

Continue through the town; bear left onto Castle Road and then left again on Corn Hill Road. It was to Corn Hill that the Pilgrims came after exploring for two days on the ocean side to signal the *Mayflower* that they were safe. Here, they reportedly found Indian corn in a cache. Legend has it that they took the corn, planted it in Plymouth and from their first harvest repaid the Indians their original measure. From the top of the hill, on a clear day, you will have a commanding view of Cape Cod Bay, and also Pamet Valley. The DAR has placed a marker on the spot where the corn was found.

HIGHLAND LIGHT

Return to Route 6 via Corn Hill and Castle Roads and turn left. Not far down Route 6, lighthouse buffs will be attracted by a sign on the right for the Cape Cod Light. At the end of Highland Road, on a 150-foot clay cliff in North Truro is Highland Light. The present lighthouse, built in 1857, is the third to be erected on this spot. The original lighthouse of 1798 gained fame as the first lighthouse on Cape Cod. The rim of the cliff offers spectacular views of the Atlantic Ocean.

HEAD-OF-THE-MEADOW BEACH

Return to Route 6, and turn right at Head-of-the Meadow Road. At the end of this road you will discover one of the loveliest stretches of natural wild beach. It is now under the protection of the National Seashore. At low tide, about 200 yards to your left, you may be able see the hull of a German bark, *The Francis*, which went aground in 1873, while transporting sugar to our shores.

SAND DUNES — PILGRIM LAKE

Leave Route 6 and proceed toward Provincetown on 6A, which has reappeared and which runs parallel to Route 6 on the Bay side of this very narrow land. On your right, you will see Pilgrim Lake rimmed by 40-to-60-foot-high sand dunes. This Pilgrim Heights Area has been deeded to the Cape Cod National Seashore and belongs to the people of the United States, a gift from the Commonwealth of Massachusetts.

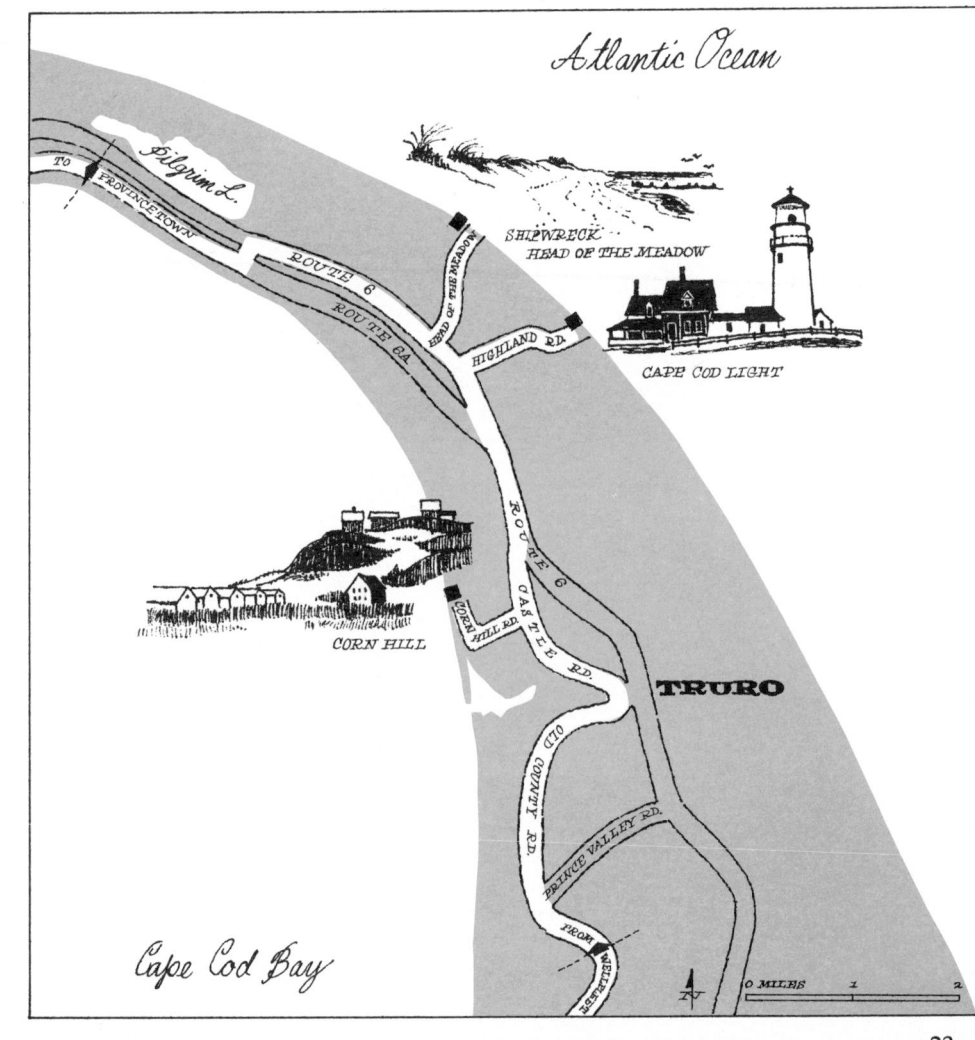

10 Provincetown

Provincetown, or "P-Town," as the Cape Codders prefer to call it, is one of the most unique towns in America, with its narrow, one-lane streets, small, erratic or nonexistent sidewalks and its little white houses sitting on pocket handkerchief-sized lots, enclosed by trim picket fences.

The area was originally a part of Truro, and was known as "Cape Cod" until 1727 when it was incorporated

under the name of Provincetown. In the early 19th century, Portuguese sailors arrived aboard whaling ships and stayed to engage in coastal fishing, later bringing their families and relatives from Portugal. Many of the year-round inhabitants today are of Portuguese heritage.

It was in this snug harbor that the Mayflower, with its weary band of 102 pilgrims, found shelter one cold day in November, 1620. They remained for an entire month, exploring the Cape before sailing on to Plymouth. Also, at this harbor, the famous Mayflower Compact, one of the first government documents in our history, was drawn up and signed. A bas-relief behind the Town Hall, in the center of the town, commemorates this agreement.

PILGRIM MONUMENT
In 1910, a 255-foot monument was dedicated in honor of the Pilgrims. The top of the Pilgrim Monument commands a view of the entire Cape, and there is a very worthwhile museum at the foot of this landmark. The remainder of this hook of land, where the high sand dunes surround the town, is called the Province Lands. They have belonged to the public since the 17th century. Massachusetts has deeded them to the National Seashore.

"P-TOWN"
Provincetown is "Mecca" for all who are interested in the Arts. Here, the Provincetown Players (organized in 1915) altered the course of theater history in America by staging plays in a fish house at the end of the pier under the auspices of such greats as Susan Glaspell and Eugene O'Neill, which brought immediate fame. There are also many art galleries, gift shops, interesting handmade craft displays and unique restaurants.

PROVINCE LANDS VISITOR CENTER

Located about two miles from Route 6 on Race Point Road, the National Seashore's Province Lands Visitor Center is the focal point of the area. From the upper deck of this building, you will discover a spectacular view over the rolling dunes to the Atlantic Ocean and Cape Cod Bay that is unsurpassed anywhere else on the Cape. The Old Harbor Life Saving Museum is visible at the end of Race Point Road. Parking and a trail make it available to the visitor. Many trails wander all through the dunes and the lovely Beech Forest. Traveling the bike trails is a rewarding experience in the Province Lands.

THE LEGEND OF MAUSHOP

The legend of how the Indians thought the Cape was formed is very entertaining. It goes like this: Many, many years ago there was a giant called Maushop who lived in the mountains. When night fell there was not enough room for the giant to stretch out. He looked off and saw in the distance a strip of sand and said, "That's the place for me." He thereupon donned his seven league boots, walked over the mountains and lay prone upon the sand.

It still wasn't long enough to accommodate all of him, so he began to push the sand ahead of him until his head came to rest in Provincetown and his feet lay resting in Woods Hole. He twisted and turned so much during the night that when he awoke in the morning, both boots were full of sand. He took off one boot, shook it out into the water and that became Martha's Vineyard. He removed the other boot, shook it over the water and that became Nantucket.

An imaginative tale, no doubt inspired by these two charming locales. Now, if you, like the Giant, will don seven league boots and "step" over Truro and Wellfleet to Eastham on Route 6, you will be headed for Route 28 and the south side of the Cape.

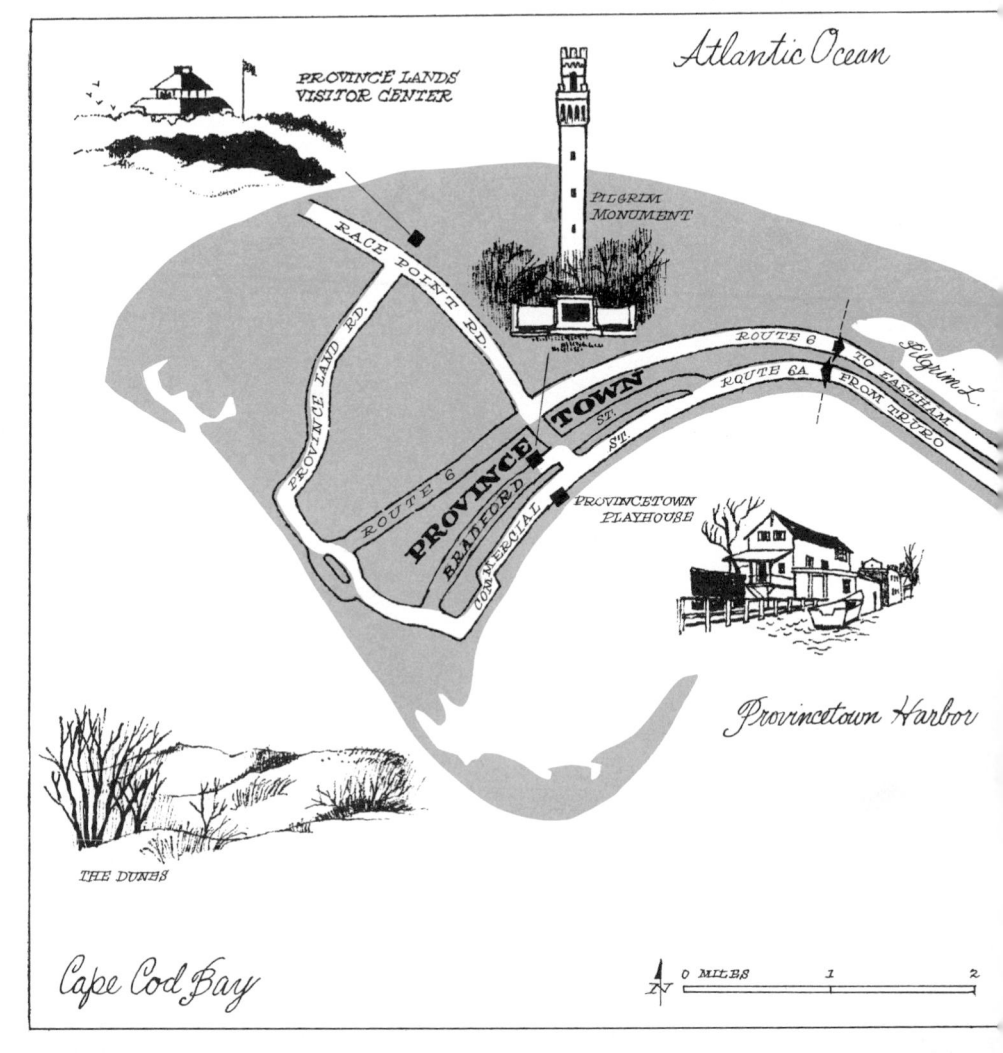

11 Eastham and Orleans again

The traffic lights at the Visitor's Center of the National Seashore in Eastham are about 25 miles from Provincetown. Continue about one and one-half miles on Route 6 to Governor Prence Road and turn left. Then bear off on Fort Hill Road and continue to the very end, where you will find a parking lot, and a vantage point to take in the breathtaking view over Nauset Marsh to the Atlantic Ocean beyond.

THE OUTERMOST HOUSE

As you look over the marsh, at the end of the beach was the house, swept to sea in 1978 where Henry Beston lived alone for a year while he wrote his famous book, *The Outermost House*. This building belonged to the Massachusetts Audubon Society. In the marsh at low tide, one may observe many varieties of marine life and shore birds.

SAMUEL de CHAMPLAIN

In the early 1600's Nauset Marsh was a sheltered cove with an open mouth to the ocean and a passageway to the Bay. Samuel de Champlain, exploring for his native France, arrived in 1605 and named the place Nauset Harbor after the tribe of Indians he found living in the hills. At this moment, you may be standing where Chief Aspinet stood over 300 years ago.

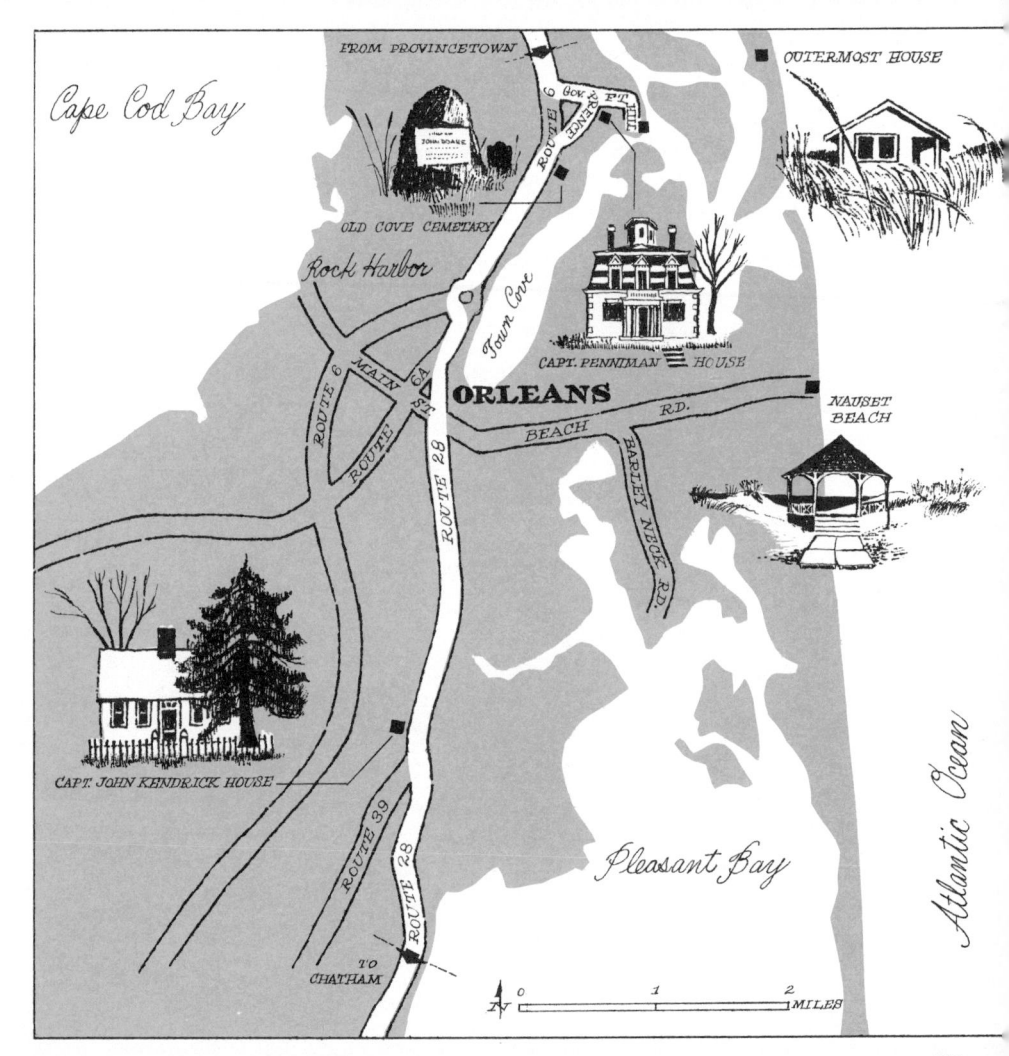

CAPTAIN PENNIMAN HOUSE

As you entered Fort Hill Road, you passed a massive yellow Victorian house on a knoll. This was built by Captain Edward Penniman in 1867 from house plans he brought from Europe. The cottonwood trees lining the driveway were grown from seedlings brought in his vest pocket from Chicago. Captain Penniman went to sea at the age of 11 and became one of the most successful whaling captains of the Lower Cape. He lived in the house until his death in 1913. It is now the property of the Cape Cod National Seashore.

OLD COVE CEMETERY

Return to Route 6 and turn left. About one quarter of a mile ahead, you will find a cemetery which contains the graves of three *Mayflower* passengers: Constance Hopkins Snow, Giles Hopkins and Lieutenant Joseph Rogers.

CAPTAIN JOHN KENDRICK

Continue to the traffic circle on Route 6, then follow Route 28 toward Chatham. About three miles beyond the traffic circle on the right, virtually hidden by huge trees, is a good example of a full Cape Cod house. It was built in 1792 by a cousin of the famous Captain John Kendrick. Captain Kendrick's ship, the *Columbia,* under the command of Robert Gray, was the first American ship to circumnavigate the globe, carrying the American flag around the world. Beyond the house, there are some seven miles of scenic driving along Pleasant Bay which will bring you to Chatham.

12 Chatham

The large tract of land between Yarmouth and Eastham was originally roamed by the Sauquatucket and the Monomoyick Indian tribes. In 1656, William Nickerson bought from Mattaquason, sachem of the Monomoyicks, that part of the tract which is now Chatham. Named "Monomoy" by Nickerson, it was one of the original plantations, not being formed out of other towns. On June 11, 1712, it was incorporated into a township and its name changed to Chatham.

"W.C.C."

Approaching Chatham on Route 28, you will pass the red brick buildings of MCI, formerly RCA. This is a communications center for ships all over the world. The call letters of the old Marconi Wireless Station, "W.C.C." are still used today.

JOSEPH LINCOLN'S HOME

When you reach the traffic lights where Route 28 turns inland, continue straight ahead for an interesting detour off 28. About one mile on your left, as you travel slowly, you will see a rambling, brown-shingled house. Although Joseph Lincoln, prolific writer of Cape Cod stories, was born in Brewster, it was here in later years that he spent his summers and wrote most of his books.

LIGHTHOUSE AND COAST GUARD STATION

About one-half mile beyond the Lincoln home you will

find Chatham Light, the Coast Guard Station and a monument dedicated to the heroism of the lifesavers of these shores. From the lookout area, you will have a dramatic view of the Atlantic Ocean.

STAGE HARBOR
Continue to the right onto Bridge Street, where you will cross a drawbridge. At the end of Bridge Street, you can turn left and proceed a short distance to an interesting stone marker. This is the spot where, in 1606, the French explorer Samuel de Champlain landed and encountered the Monomoyick Indians.

ATWOOD HOUSE
A right turn at the end of Bridge Street will bring you to the Atwood House. This is the oldest house in Chatham, dating back to 1752. It is now the home of the Chatham Historical Society and a museum.

FISHING SHANTIES
Continue straight ahead to rejoin Route 28 at the traffic circle. Turn left heading west again until you reach Barn Hill Road on the left, just before the Shop Ahoy shopping area in West Chatham. Turn left on Barn Hill Road and continue to the water, where you will find a typical Old Cape scene. Nestled at the foot of a high bluff are oyster shacks with the Oyster River lapping at the doors; fishermen in traditional yellow oilskins shucking oysters; and gulls screaming overhead as they wait for tidbits.

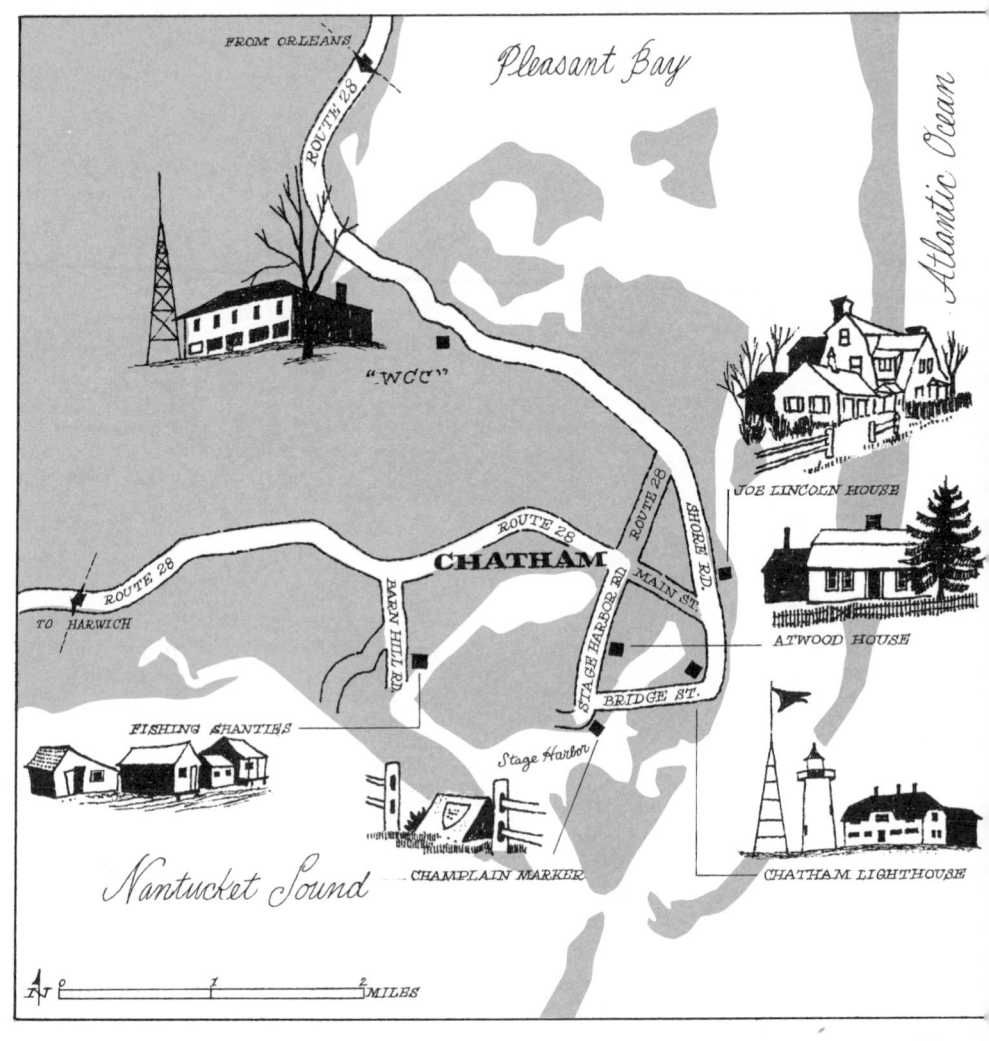

13 Harwich

Back on Route 28, you will next come upon Harwich, a town made up of seven villages. Incorporated in 1694, it had the largest land area of any Cape town until 1797, when a portion was set off for what is now South Orleans. In 1803, another section was set aside for what is now Brewster.

SOUTH HARWICH

This is the village you enter as you cross the Chatham-Harwich line. In the early days, it was a bustling place with several factories and a large mackerel fleet which tied up at the end of Deep Hole Road.

WYCHMERE HARBOR

On the left, off Route 28 in Harwich Port, is Wychmere Harbor, one of the snuggest and most picturesque anchorages on the south side of the Cape. Originally, this harbor was a pond with only a small creek leading to the ocean. As late as 1900, there was a race track for trotters around the pond.

CRANBERRY BOGS

Just beyond Wychmere Harbor, make a right on Freeman Street, which joins Bank Street, for about a mile's drive inland to Harwich Center. A short distance past the junction of Freeman and Bank Streets on the right, you will see the large cranberry bogs. It was in Harwich, in the 1840's, that the first bog was planted for commercially grown cranberries.

BROOKS BLOCK

The entire building houses the Brooks Free Library, well worth a visit.

1812 CANNON

At the entrance to Brooks Park, where you will be obliged to turn around, you will see two cannons; the larger came from a British frigate during the War of 1812. You are now moving west on Main Street under beautiful elm trees. On your right, you will see the Congregational Church, whose graceful spire and distinctive architecture exemplifies New England churches.

BROOKS ACADEMY

Diagonally across from the church is an edifice known

as the Brooks Academy Building, the first school of navigation. It was called Pine Grove Seminary when it was built in 1844 by Sidney Brooks. Subsequently, it was used as a public school. Today, it houses the Harwich Historical Society.

Concerning navigation, there is the story of an old sailmaker who built boats in the summer and coffins in the winter, and who, between seasons, was known to imbibe a bit. One October day, a town official expired and the sailmaker was approached for a coffin. It was his imbibing period, but he was nevertheless prevailed upon to make the coffin. He said it would be ready in a day or two, and it was. It was beautifully done, but when the lid was removed, there, smack down the middle, was a centerboard!

OLD POWDER HOUSE

In front of the Brooks Academy building, which, by the way, is a fine example of Greek Revival architecture, stands a small building where gunpowder once was stored by the town's militia to be used in wars, 1776-1860.

MORE CRANBERRY BOGS

Out of Harwich Center, you can take Route 124 about one and a quarter miles north if you wish to see the beautiful cranberry bogs surrounding Pleasant Lake. Harvesting time is usually in September and October. From 1844 until about 1960, the berries were picked by men, women and children who crept along on their knees, taking the berries off the vines in the bogs with cranberry scoops. Today, most of the bogs are machine-harvested.

Return to Harwich Center, turn right at the church and proceed straight ahead on Main Street. Bear left at the fork and continue on Great Western Road for a refreshing ride through pine woods to South Dennis.

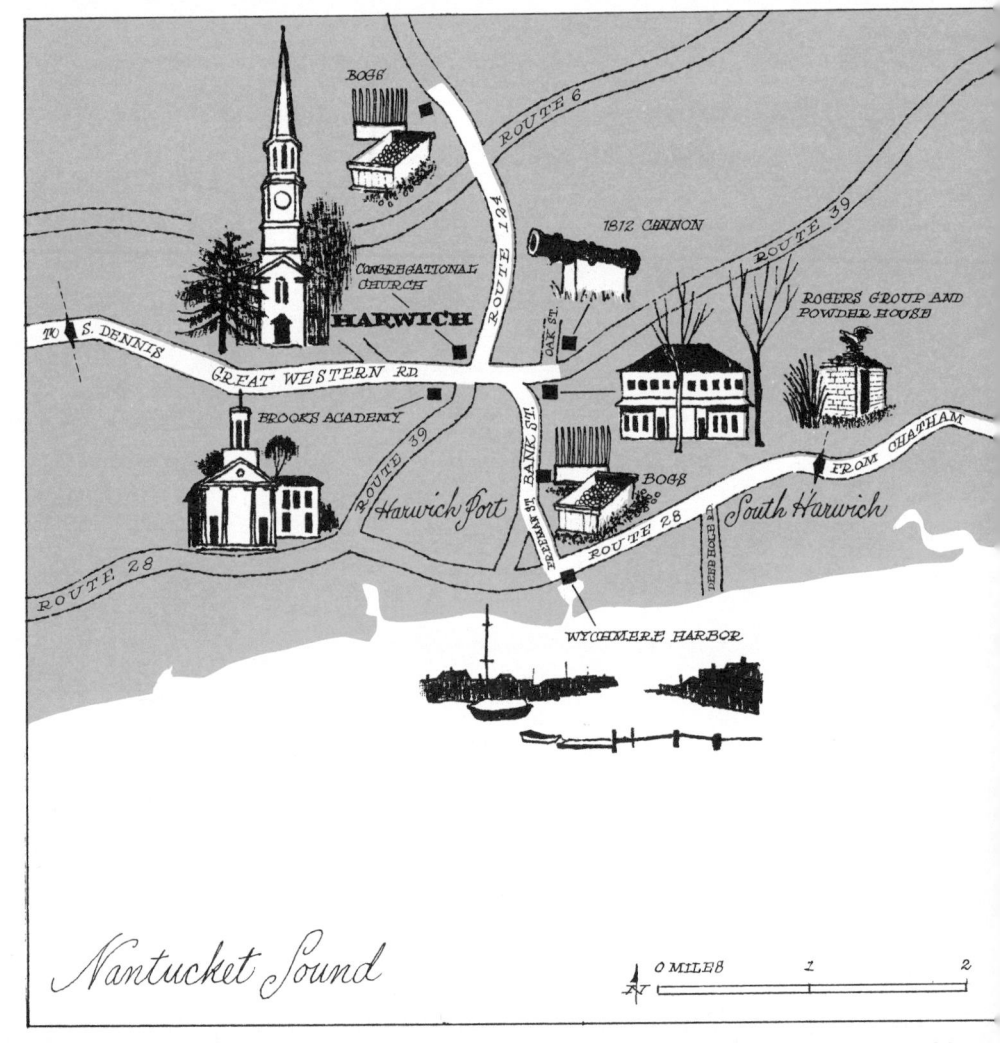

Nantucket Sound

34

14 South Dennis

Drive along the Great Western Road for about five miles and at its conclusion, turn right to the traffic lights. Cross Route 134, and then bear left at a fork in the road. At the next crossroad, turn left on Main Street to get your first view of the quaint little village of South Dennis, situated in the middle of the Cape. You will pass a small white country church, the South Dennis Congregational Church. It is believed that this church has the oldest pipe organ in this country.

"JERICHO"

After leaving the church, continue on this road, which rejoins Route 28, and you will drive by the "Jericho" House. This is an old sea captain's home which now belongs to the Dennis Historical Society. The name "Jericho" was given to it by Elizabeth Reynard, author of *The Narrow Land*.

SOUTH YARMOUTH – BASS RIVER

Back on Route 28 you will cross Bass River. Some historians believe that the Norsemen sailed this river inland as far as Follins Pond in South Dennis. It is possible that they remained in the area for some time.

For a scenic drive along Bass River, turn left at the traffic lights and take the first left; then, the first right. You will pass many beautiful homes along this river road. Shortly, you will travel inland, but if you continue to bear left you will arrive at the water again, and eventually the road will rejoin Route 28. At this point, a left turn will carry you toward Hyannis.

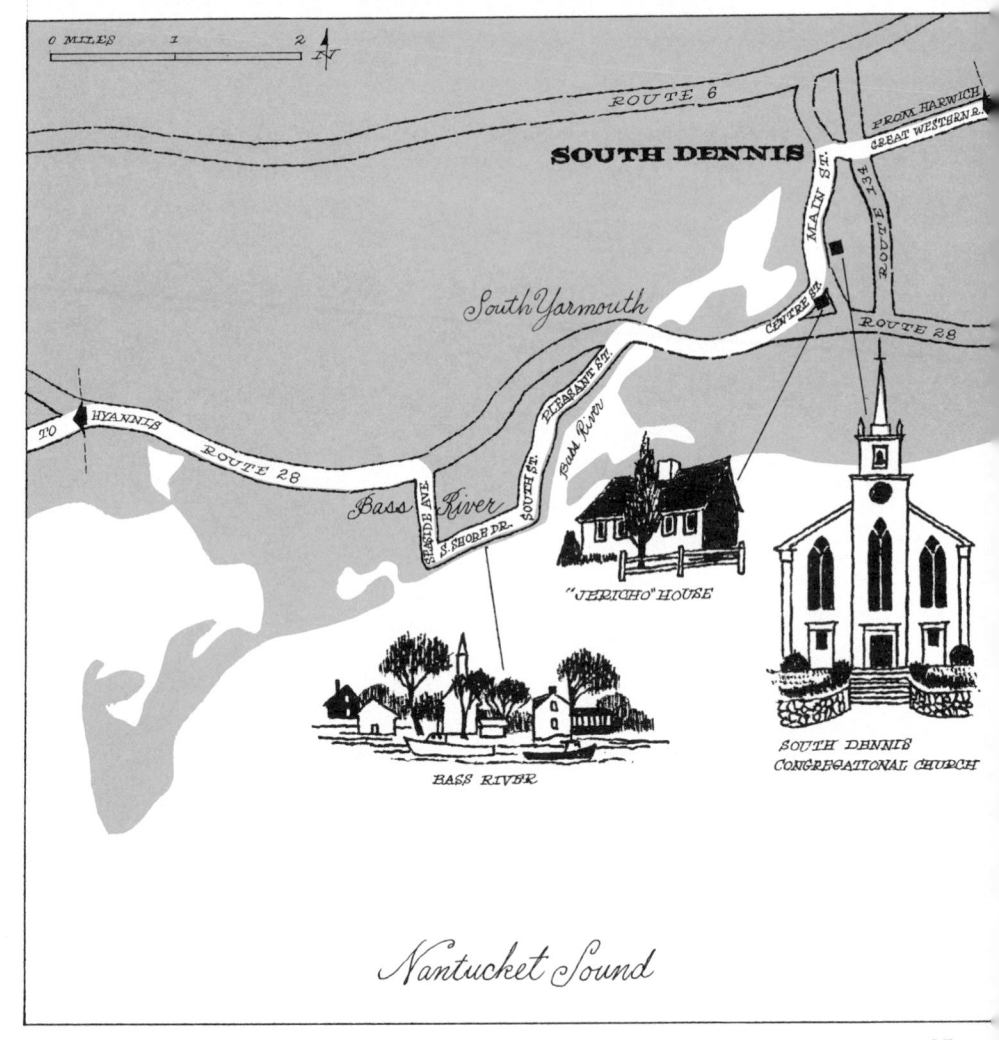

"JERICHO" HOUSE

SOUTH DENNIS CONGREGATIONAL CHURCH

BASS RIVER

Nantucket Sound

The town of Barnstable includes a number of villages, of which Hyannis is just one; but Hyannis, with its busy Main Street, its stores, restaurants and motels, has become the "city" of the Cape. It is a transportation center with a fine airport. In the summer, boats leave regularly for Nantucket and Martha's Vineyard.

KENNEDY MEMORIAL

On Main Street, in the center of Hyannis, head west through the shopping area to Sea Street. Turn left, and proceed on Sea Street to Gosnold Street (about one mile) and turn left. Gosnold Street will take you to Ocean Street and the John F. Kennedy Memorial. Return on Gosnold Street to Sea Street, turn left and continue toward Hyannisport.

HYANNISPORT

Cape Cod has the honor of harboring the summer residences of two presidents; Grover Cleveland who summered at Gray Gables in Bourne from 1891 to 1904; and John F. Kennedy, who came to the Cape throughout his boyhood to his death in 1963. Visitors are not permitted near the Kennedy home, but they can pass close enough to see the large sprawling houses which comprise the "Kennedy Compound."

CRAIGVILLE BEACH

Leaving the Kennedy area, proceed to Centerville by way of Craigville Beach. This is one of the largest public beaches on the Cape and one of the loveliest. A minister settled the community of Craigville and started Christian Camp Meetings for a group of fellow ministers. Later, the group purchased the 800-foot strip of land which is now Craigville Beach.

CENTERVILLE

The beautiful little community of Centerville, not far from Craigville Beach, is filled with delightful old houses bordered by spacious lawns, shaded by stately elm trees. The Centerville Historical Society, in the Mary Lincoln House on Main Street, features an interesting display of wedding gowns of early-to-present vintage. At the light, in the center of the village, you will see the signs directing you to Osterville.

OSTERVILLE

Osterville, to boat lovers, is a name synonymous with the Crosby Cat Boat. Horace Crosby designed the first "Cat" in about 1850, and although boat designing has changed radically, the Crosby Boat Yard is still in operation. Osterville serves as the shopping center for nearby Wianno and Oyster Harbors. In these two communities, you will find magnificent homes surrounded by well-tended gardens.

COTUIT

Cotuit, at one time, was famous for its oysters. "Cotuits on the half-shell" were featured in restaurants all over the world, although many of the oysters probably never saw these waters at all. In 1820, Cotuit boasted a large fleet of vessels; now it is a snug port for the summer sailboats that dot the sound. Also, in 1820, when the first need for a burial ground arose, it was prepared in great haste. The epitaph on the first headstone reads:

"My Bosom friend, come here to see
Where lays the last remains of me.
When I the debt to nature paid,
A burying ground for me was made."

This cemetery is one of the most beautiful to be found on the Cape today.

As you leave Cotuit, you will in effect be leaving the town of Barnstable, of which Hyannis, Hyannisport, Centerville, Osterville and Cotuit are village components. Return to Route 28 to continue to Mashpee.

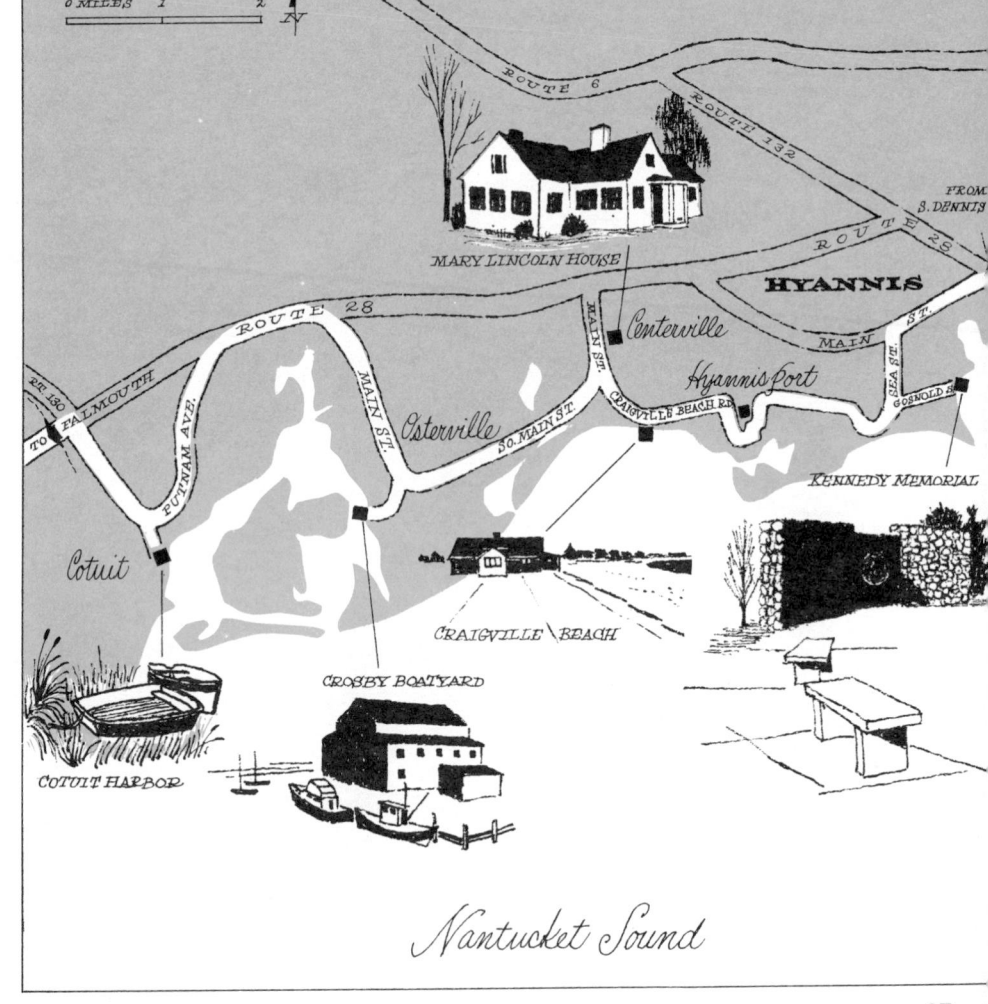

16   Mashpee, Falmouth & Bourne

Mashpee, predominantly inland, is named for the tribe of Indians which settled here long before the white man ever heard of Cape Cod. They lived among the stately trees, or along the many ponds abounding with fish, ponds which have since catered to such famous fishermen as President Grover Cleveland, Daniel Webster, and the famous actor of his day, Joseph Jefferson. Mashpee also has the distinction of being the first Indian Reservation in this country. That the

Indians retained any land at all is no doubt due to the efforts of their first minister and champion, Richard Bourne.

INDIAN CHURCH

On Route 28, one finds the only remaining monument to Richard Bourne — an old Indian Church. Built in 1684 on his own land, it was moved to its present site in 1717. From 1711 until recent times, ministers of the church were paid by a fund entrusted to Harvard College. Until 1932, Indian ceremonial rituals were held in secrecy. Today, the public is invited to attend these summer rituals.

FALMOUTH

Falmouth, with its great complex of Otis Air Force Base, is the second "city" on the Cape. Even with such growth, Falmouth retains much of its early charm. It also is one of the few Cape towns which has kept its boundaries intact throughout the years. In the early days, Falmouth was known as Suckanessett. In Indian, "Suckaness" means "home of the black clam." The suffix "et" or "ett" on an Indian name was used to denote "by the water." Therefore, Suckanessett translated: "Home of the black clam by the water."

Falmouth was once a great fishing and whaling port. The stately old homes surrounding the beautiful Village Green are evidence of the affluence of the early captains. Many of these huge, square houses have the widow's walk enclosures — little fenced — in platforms on the rooftops — where wives of the whalers watched for the return of their seafaring husbands. As the name suggests, many never returned.

An outstanding example of such a house is the one on the Green alongside the Congregational Church. The belfry of the church contains a bell made by Paul Revere, one of the few Revere bells still being rung today. Nearby, in another of the stately square houses — painted yellow — is the Falmouth Historical Museum. Also near the Village Green, on the road to Woods Hole, is the birthplace of Katherine Lee Bates, who wrote the hymn *America, the Beautiful*.

WOODS HOLE

If Provincetown at one end of the Cape is considered the art center, Woods Hole at the other end is renowned today as an important scientific community. Virtually every country in the world is now involved in research carried out here.

In the early 1800's, Woods Hole with its deep, well-sheltered harbor gained prominence as a whaling and shipbuilding village. In 1859, the Pacific Guano

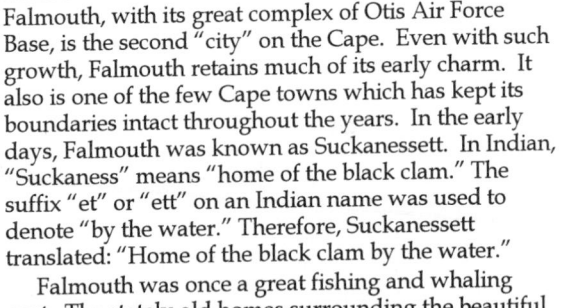

Company started a fertilizer processing plant here, transporting the raw guano by ship around Cape Horn from islands off the west coast of South America. In 1873, the great scientist, Louis Agassis, began working here and from that time it has expanded into a major research center. During the latter part of the century, several other chemical laboratories were also established here. Woods Hole contains the Marine Biological Laboratory; the Woods Hole Oceanographic Institution; and the U.S. Fish and Wildlife Service. The latter maintains an excellent aquarium, open to the public during the summer months.

Ferryboats, carrying both cars and foot passengers, leave at regularly scheduled intervals (all year round) for Martha's Vineyard and Nantucket. If you make a sharp right on Church Street as you leave Woods Hole, you can return to Falmouth via one of the rare oceanside routes along the Cape. You may wish to pause at the bluff where Nobska Lighthouse stands.

BOURNE

From Falmouth, head north on Rte. 28 to Bourne. Until 1884, Bourne was part of Sandwich. It was not named, as many suppose, for Richard Bourne but for a descendant of his, Jonathan Bourne. The town of Bourne is divided by the Cape Cod Canal, with some of its villages located on the "mainland." It was in 1627 that Miles Standish first conceived the idea of building a canal in this area, in order to make trading with the Dutch easier. Ironically, it was not until much later, in 1909, that the first spadeful of dirt was removed to start the canal. In 1914, the canal was opened for the passage of vessels, and in 1928, was purchased by the Federal Government.

TWO ENTERPRISES

Two businesses, one of which is still in existence, had their beginnings in Bourne. Swift & Company, of Chicago, maintained a slaughterhouse in West Sandwich (now Bourne). The Keith Car Manufacturing Company, a blacksmith shop in 1834, produced the "prairie schooners" in which men such as John Sutter traveled west for the California gold rush. Later, the company produced wooden freight cars.

APTUCXET TRADING POST

Leave Route 28 at the sign of Trading Post Corner and Monument Beach. This will take you to the Trading Post Corner, also known as Five Corners. Here you will see the sign for Aptucxet Trading Post. The Indian translation of Aptucxet is: "at the little trap river." It refers to the river which has now been widened into the Cape Cod Canal. In 1927, a replica of the old Aptucxet Trading Post, built 300 years earlier for trade between the New Amsterdam Dutch and the colony at Plymouth, was built. It is now a museum. Wampum made from the quahog shell or strings of periwinkle shells were considered legal tender until about 1661. Six pieces of quahog were equivalent to one English penny.

The Aptucxet Trading Post is open from May to Mid-October.

As you leave this quiet, 17th-century atmosphere to return to the 20th-century Bourne Bridge and modern roads, your tour of Cape Cod will be complete. There is one last legend about the Cape that is appropriate here: "Once the sand of Cape Cod gets into your shoes, you are never free of it, and you will return." And each time, Cape Cod will welcome and charm you anew.

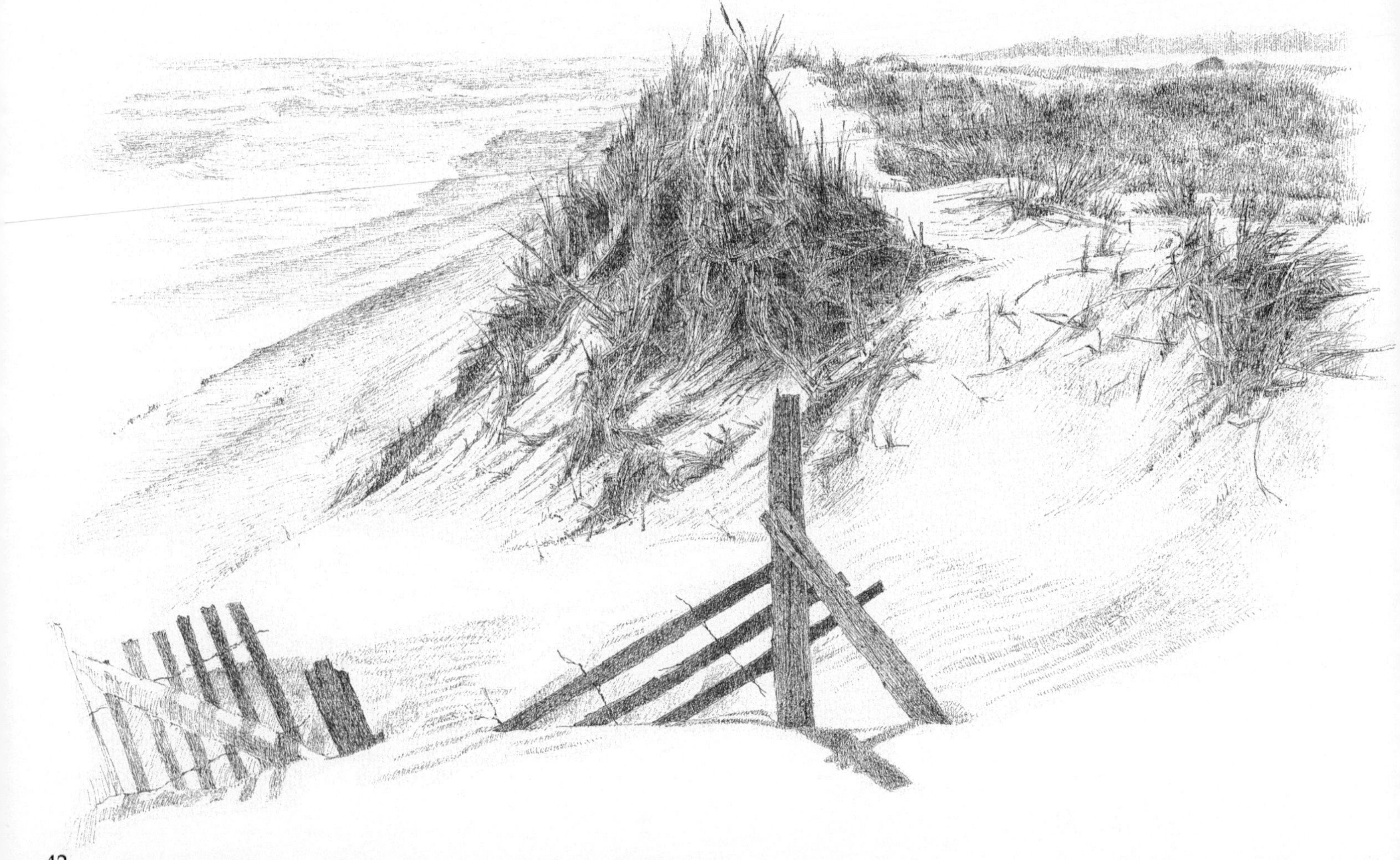

A Portfolio of Old Cape Cod Drawings by Richard Fish

Right: A rowboat from yesterday resting in the marsh grass near Rock Harbor.

A front approaches
Nauset Marsh

44

The Captain Penniman House
on Fort Hill Road in Eastham

Index

DORIS DOANE

Doris Doane traces her ancestry to Deacon John Doane who settled in Eastham in 1644. She married into another branch of the Doane family; currently, including two grandchildren, there have been twelve generations of Doanes.

As a former librarian at the Harwichport Library Mrs. Doane pursued an interest in Doane genealogy as well as the history and folklore of Cape Cod. She is a past president of the Harwich Historical Society and the Garden Club of Harwich. Mrs. Doane attended Cape schools and State Teachers College at Bridgewater. She is the author of *A Book of Cape Cod Houses*, illustrated by Howard Rich (Chatham Press).

Among her many accomplishments during twelve years as Supervisor of Salt Pond Visitors Center, Cape Cod National Seashore, one close to her heart is her design and development of the award-winning trail for the blind in Eastham, Massachusetts.

Mrs. Doane retired to a busy schedule as a noted lecturer on Cape Cod, its history and architecture. She resides in Harwich.

RICHARD FISH

Richard Fish, a Pennsylvania native and graduate of the Philadelphia College of Art and the University of Pennsylvania, has been awarded numerous citations for paintings, drawings and graphic design. His work has been shown at Butler Institute of American Art, Delaware Art Museum, Philadelphia Museum of Art, Comer Gallery of Art and others. Richard Fish's paintings are represented in many collections in this country and abroad.

A noted illustrator of books, his work appears in "Magic Realism" (Society of Illustrators), "Life and Death of The Salt Marsh" (Atlantic Little Brown), "Return to Big Grass" (Ducks Unlimited), "One Day in Summer" (Random House), "East of America" (Chatham Press), and in publications such as *International Wildlife, Atlantic Monthly, New York Times, Readers Digest* and *Yankee* magazine.

Mr. Fish's work reflects his interests and experiences as artist-in-residence at Rocky Mountain National Park, his many visits to the Outer Hebrides of Scotland, and his visits to the U.S. Southwest. Yet, through the years, Cape Cod has always held the center of his affection.